SINGER'S LIBRARY OF MUSICAL THEATRE

35 SONGS FROM THE BROADWAY STAGE

35 PIANO ACCOMPANIMENT TRACKS ENCLOSED!

A TREASURY OF MUSICAL THEATRE SONGS IN THEIR ORIGINAL KEYS, SELECTED BY VOCAL RANGE. AUTHENTIC ARRANGEMENTS TRANSCRIBED FROM ORIGINAL VOCAL SCORES, WITH SPECIALLY RECORDED PIANO ACCOMPANIMENTS ON TWO CDs.

PIANO RECORDINGS
BY BARBARA IRVINE AND DENNIS BUCK

RECORDINGS PRODUCED BY BILL GALLIFORD

RECORDED AND MIXED BY JUAN CRISTOBAL AND
ALFONSO ORDOÑEZ AT SONIC PROJECTS INC.

Alfred Music Publishing Co., Inc.
16320 Roscoe Blvd., Suite 100
P.O. Box 10003
Van Nuys, CA 91410-0003
alfred.com

(800) 876-9777
10075 SW Beav-Hills Hwy (503) 641-5691
1010 SE Powell (503) 775-0800
12334 SE Division (503) 760-6881

Book only (26541)
ISBN-10: 0-7390-4473-7
ISBN-13: 978-0-7390-4473-5

2 CDs only (32767)
ISBN-10: 0-7390-6095-3
ISBN-13: 978-0-7390-6095-7

Book & 2 CDs (32766)
ISBN-10: 0-7390-6094-5
ISBN-13: 978-0-7390-6094-0

Cover Photos
Curtains: © iStockphoto.com / tobkatrina • Manhattan skyline: © iStockphoto.com / BRANDONJ74

Contents

Handwritten: 9/28/17

Introduction

When Alfred Publishing asked me to write the text for this series, I welcomed the opportunity to include elements that are missing from other similar collections. Within the opening pages, you will find a synopsis of the plot, the context of the song in each show, the name of the cast member who sang the song in the original production, song type, suggested 16-bar cuts, as well as the standard information such as the show creators, and the dates and theaters of the New York runs. The vocal range for each song can be found in the table of contents. Below are some helpful hints for the singing actor.

Choosing a Song for an Audition

When choosing a song to sing for an audition, ask yourself the following:

1. *Would I ever play the role of the character singing this song?* If not, but you want to sing the song anyway, find a way to make it your own; create your own context after being fully informed about the original context.

2. *Does this song show off my vocal range?* Use the vocal ranges in the table of contents to quickly identify the highest and lowest notes in each song and to determine if they are notes you can sing comfortably.

3. *Is this song appropriate for the show for which I am auditioning?* Use the dates of the first run of each show to determine its era, then compare the era of the song to the era of the show for which you are auditioning; songs from the same era are often similar in style. But, also remember that some later composers write in the style of a previous era or write in various styles. Therefore, if you listen to a recording of the show for which you are auditioning and then listen to the songs you might choose, you can determine if the styles are similar. Singing a song from another show by the same composer who wrote the show for which you are auditioning, can be an even better way to go. If the character who sings your audition song is similar to the character for which you are auditioning, that will help the people on the other side of the table better

imagine you in the role. Also, be sure that the song type complies with what is requested in the audition notice.

4. *How do I know if this song is the right type?* Audition notices often ask for a ballad, an uptempo number, a patter song, a comedy number, standard Broadway, legit musical theatre, etc. We have suggested song-type categories for each song. Though a single song may often fall into more than one category, our type categories will serve as a helpful guide.

5. *The audition notice asks for 16 bars; which 16 bars should I sing?* There are many possibilities within each song for usable 16-bar sections. We have suggested one or two possibilities for each song that make some sense in terms of the music and the lyrics, and will show range. But, remember to always learn the entire song; you may be asked to go back and sing all of it after singing your 16 bars.

Have fun at your audition! The time is yours; own it.

The Bottom Line

There is no substitute for a good vocal coach. Go to him or her with your ideas based on the above suggestions, and he or she can then hone in on what will be best for you.

—Barbara Irvine

Barbara Irvine lived in New York City for 15 years, working as a music director/vocal coach/pianist/music copyist/arranger/transcriber/transposer. She has worked with nearly all the major Broadway composers of her time there, as well as with many of the Broadway stars.

Notes

Warning: the paragraphs about the shows may contain plot spoilers.

Any actor mentioned as having originally played a role is from the opening-night cast, unless otherwise indicated.

Some of the suggested 16-bar cuts are slightly longer or shorter than exactly 16 bars in order to create complete sections. Most often, these cuttings will still be accepted at auditions asking for 16 bars. You might choose to use a bar or two preceding the cut as an introduction, or simply ask the audition pianist for a "bell tone" to use as your starting pitch; the latter is more customary and time saving. Bar numbers are indicated as m. #, e. g. bar 16 is indicated as m. 16.

110 in the Shade

The Show

Following the success of Off-Broadway's *The Fantasticks*, this was Schmidt and Jones's first Broadway production. The show was adapted from N. Richard Nash's play *The Rainmaker*, in which a drought-stricken town in the early American West is taken in by an alleged rainmaker named Bill Starbuck. Unprepossessing town resident Lizzie Curry is attracted to Starbuck but is unimpressed by his rainmaking claims. Their friendship progresses to a physical level, but when Starbuck asks Lizzie to join him in his travels, she chooses to remain at home and continue her relationship with suitor Sheriff File. Alas, the rain does come by the end of the show.

The Authors

Music by Harvey Schmidt; Lyrics by Tom Jones; Book by N. Richard Nash

New York Runs

October 24, 1963–August 9, 1964: Broadhurst Theatre

July 25, 1992–November 15, 1992: New York City Opera (12 performances, including one preview)

May 9, 2007–the present: Studio 54

The Songs

"Love, Don't Turn Away" CD 2 / TRACK 1

Lizzie (originated by Inga Swenson, played by Karen Ziemba in the NYCO production and by Audra McDonald in the Broadway revival) sings "Love, Don't Turn Away" when, after her failed trip to meet a man, her brothers and father decide to invite the eligible bachelor, Sheriff File, to the annual picnic. In this song, Lizzie is alone, imagining what it would be like to get herself all fixed up for a man.

Song Type

standard Broadway (This moderate tempo song lies somewhere between a ballad and an uptempo song. It would be an appropriate choice when only one song is required.)

Suggested 16-Bar Cuts for Auditions

m. 45 (without the pickup) through m. 56 +
m. 65 through m. 70

m. 57 (without the pickup) through m. 70

"Simple Little Things" CD 2 / TRACK 11

"Simple Little Things" is sung by Lizzie when she realizes that, in spite of the fireworks she feels with Starbuck and the dreams he tries to instill in her, the simple things are what she really wants.

Song Type

standard Broadway/ballad

Suggested 16-Bar Cut for Auditions

m. 45 through m. 56

"Is It Really Me?" CD 1 / TRACK 14

Swept off her feet by Starbuck, and believing for the first time that she is truly beautiful, Lizzie sings "Is It Really Me?" at Starbuck's wagon. Shortly after this, he confesses that he is a con man.

Song Type

standard Broadway/ballad

Suggested 16-Bar Cuts for Auditions

m. 25 through m. 40

m. 18 through m. 29 + m. 34 through
m. 38 + m. 40

Babes in Arms

The Show

This show contains more stand-alone hits than any other Rodgers and Hart musical: "I Wish I Were in Love Again," "Johnny One Note," "The Lady Is a Tramp," "My Funny Valentine," "Where or When." The 1937 production involved a group of teenagers whose vaudevillian parents are on the road. A local sheriff wants to send the idle youngsters to a work farm, so they decide to put on a show to prove their worth. They succeed, but not without some difficulties, romance, and perseverance. Alfred Drake made his Broadway debut in this show as well as Dan Dailey. In 1959, George Oppenheimer, under Richard Rodgers's supervision, revised the script. In this later version, a group of poor, young apprentices are working at the Surf and Sand Playhouse in Cape Cod. Together, they have written a revue which they hope will raise money to help theatre co-owner Bunny buy out her not-so-nice partner, Seymour Fleming. Fleming tries to thwart the apprentices' plan by putting on a horrible play called *The Deep North*. The apprentices sabotage his play with miscues and crashing props. They then succeed in enticing Steve Edwards, a young producer, away from Fleming's play to the barn where they perform their revue for him. Edwards options their show, and that money enables Bunny to gain full control of her theatre. A film entitled *Babes in Arms* was made in 1939 featuring Mickey Rooney and Judy Garland. The film plot bore little resemblance to that of the original stage musical and retained only two of the Rodgers and Hart songs, "Babes in Arms" and "Where or When."

The Authors

Music by Richard Rodgers; Lyrics by Lorenz Hart; Book by Richard Rodgers and Lorenz Hart

New York Run

April 14, 1937–December 18, 1937: Shubert Theatre (to October, 1937); Majestic Theatre (10/25/37–12/18/37)

The Song

"The Lady Is a Tramp" CD 1 / TRACK 15

Phyllis Owen, the mother of young actress Jennifer Owen, has insulted Bunny, telling her she should be more ladylike. After Owen leaves, Bunny tells some of the apprentices that she is a different kind of lady in "The Lady Is a Tramp". (The character named Billie Smith [played by Mitzi Green] sang this song in the 1937 production.)

Song Type

standard Broadway/uptempo

Suggested 16-Bar Cuts for Auditions

m. 26 through m. 37 + m. 70 through m. 72 + m. 81

m. 26 through m. 37 + m. 74 through m. 81

Babes in Toyland

The Show

Considered an operetta by most, the plot of this musical resembles the plot of *The Wizard of Oz*, containing a storm, a scary journey, and a fantastical city. Orphans Alan and Jane, the two "babes," live with their evil Uncle Barnaby, who wants to do away with them so that he can obtain their inherited fortune. His first attempt fails, and instead of drowning in the shipwreck he arranged, the orphans end up in Toyland where they experience many adventures with Mother Goose characters. When the orphans return to Uncle Barnaby, he prepares poison for them, which he accidentally drinks himself. Alan and Jane are left to enjoy their wealth without Barnaby's interference. There was a 1934 film version, titled *The March of the Wooden Soldiers*, which used only five of the original songs and very little of the original book, starring Laurel and Hardy. A 1961 movie, starring Ed Wynn and Ray Bolger, had a revised plot, but included many of the original songs with lyrics and tempi that differed from the Broadway versions. There have been three television adaptations, as well as a Disney animated version that was released in

1997. Beginning in the 1970s, a version of *Babes in Toyland* in which Alan and Jane run away from home to Toyland because their parents do not pay enough attention to them, played annually at the Light Opera of Manhattan off Broadway.

The Authors

Music by Victor Herbert; Lyrics and Book by Glen MacDonough

New York Runs

October 13, 1903–March 19, 1904: Majestic Theatre (not the Majestic Theatre of today, but an earlier one that was located on the west side of Columbus Circle and was demolished in 1954)

January 2, 1905–January 21, 1905: Majestic Theatre

December 23, 1929–January 11, 1930: Jolson's 59th Street Theatre

December 20, 1930–January 1931: Imperial Theatre

The Song

"I Can't Do the Sum" CD 1 / TRACK 9

"I Can't Do the Sum" was sung by Jane (first played by Mabel Barrison) and Widow Piper's children, as they incant nonsense math problems and tap the rhythm on their slates.

Song Type

uptempo/comic/patter★

(★*if sung more quickly than the tempo marking indicates*)

Suggested 16-Bar Cuts for Auditions

m. 5 (with pickup) through m. 20 + m. 25 through m. 26 + m. 29 through m. 30 + m. 34 through m. 40 (Because this song moves fairly quickly, you can probably get away with singing more than 16 bars. Pick your favorite verse and have fun!)

m. 25 through m. 40 (This cut isn't as funny.)

The Show

Based on Shakespeare's *The Comedy of Errors*, this slightly risqué show takes place in ancient Ephesus in Asia Minor. It is the story of the adventures of two young men from Syracuse, Antipholus and his servant Dromio, who seek to find their long-lost twin brothers, who, amusingly and confusingly, bear their same names. They find them in Ephesus. Predictably, the wives of the Ephesians, Adriana and Luce, mistake the boys from Syracuse for their husbands. A 1940 film version of the show, with the score considerably changed, starred Allan Jones and Martha Raye. The Canadian Broadcasting Corporation produced a TV movie of the musical in 1986.

The Authors

Music by Richard Rodgers; Lyrics by Lorenz Hart; Book by George Abbott

New York Runs

November 23, 1938–June 10, 1939: Alvin Theatre

April 15, 1963–June 28, 1984: Theatre Four (Off-Broadway)

August 18, 2002–October 20, 2002: American Airlines Theatre

The Song

"Falling in Love with Love" CD 1 / TRACK 3

Adriana (originally played on Broadway by Muriel Angelus, later by Lauren Mitchell, and in the 1940 movie by Irene Harvey), asks her sister, Luciana, where her husband, Antipholus of Ephesus, is. She then angrily advises Luciana to avoid romance in "Falling in Love with Love."

Song Type

standard Broadway/uptempo

Suggested 16-Bar Cuts for Auditions

m. 101 through m. 122 (with accompanist holding a C major chord under m. 122)

m. 157 through m. 172 (shows higher vocal range)

Camelot

The Show

Based on T. H. White's *The Once and Future King*, a retelling of the legend of King Arthur, *Camelot* is about the Knights of the Round Table in the time of chivalry and the romantic triangle made up of Arthur, his Queen Guenevere, and a new member of the Round Table, Sir Lancelot. Guenevere comes to Camelot to marry Arthur. The idealistic Arthur has learned from the wizard Merlyn the value of peace and brotherhood, and Arthur subsequently establishes the Round Table. The young French knight Lancelot hears of the Round Table and arrives to become a member. Arthur introduces him to Guenevere, and eventually a romance develops between her and the knight. Mordred, Arthur's illegitimate son, plots to steal the throne away from his father. Throughout, Arthur strives to maintain peace at all costs, especially to himself. The movie was made in 1967 starring Richard Harris, Vanessa Redgrave, and Franco Nero. A recent U.S. tour of the show starred Michael York as Arthur, James Barbour as Lancelot, and Rachel York as Guenevere.

The Authors

Music by Frederick Loewe; Lyrics and Book by Alan Jay Lerner

New York Runs

December 3, 1960–January 5, 1963: Majestic Theatre

July 8, 1980–August 23, 1980: New York State Theatre

November 15, 1981–January 2, 1982: Winter Garden Theatre

June 21, 1993–August 7, 1993: George Gershwin Theatre

The Songs

"The Simple Joys of Maidenhood"
CD 2 / TRACK 10

In "The Simple Joys of Maidenhood," Guenevere (originally played by Julie Andrews) laments the loss of a simpler time as she contemplates her upcoming marriage to King Arthur.

Song Type

standard Broadway/ballad or uptempo depending upon which section you sing (see cuts below)

Suggested 16-Bar Cuts for Auditions

uptempo cut = m. 16 (with pickup) through m. 31

ballad cut = m. 111 through m. 134

"I Loved You Once in Silence"
CD 1 / TRACK 12
"I Loved You Once in Silence" (optional scene) CD 1 / TRACK 13

"I Loved You Once in Silence" is sung by Guenevere to Sir Lancelot when he comes to her chambers. On this night, Arthur is trapped in the forest by his conniving illegitimate son and his son's sorceress aunt.

Song Type

standard Broadway/ballad

Suggested 16-Bar Cut for Auditions

m. 45 (with pickup) through m. 65

The Fantasticks

The Show

The longest-running musical in theatre history, this show is an adaptation of the story told in the 1894 play *Les Romanesques* by Edmond Rostand. Through the conventions of *commedia dell'arte*, combined with traditions from Noh theatre, we see two fathers who conspire to make their children, Matt and Luisa, respectively, fall in love. They do so by feigning a rivalry between themselves, trusting in the classic expectation that young people will do the opposite of what they think their parents want them to do. The fathers then hire some men to stage the kidnapping of Luisa so they could appear to reconcile over their collective concern for her, and so that Matt could prove his manhood by rescuing her. Eventually, the fathers' scheme is revealed, and Matt leaves home in anger. He finally returns to Luisa and she takes him back, gladly. A 1995 feature film version starred Joel Grey, Barnard Hughes, Joey McIntyre, and Jean Louisa Kelly.

The Authors

Music by Harvey Schmidt; Lyrics and Book by Tom Jones

New York Runs

May 3, 1960–January 13, 2002: Sullivan Street Playhouse

August 23, 2006–present: Snapple Theater Center

The Song

"Much More" CD 2 / TRACK 5

"Much More" is sung by Luisa (originally played by Rita Gardner, and by Jean Louisa Kelly in the movie) to express her curiosity about the outside world, now that she has become a young woman.

Song Type

standard Broadway/uptempo

Suggested 16-Bar Cut for Auditions

m. 42 (with pickup) through m. 57

Finian's Rainbow

The Show

Based on an idea of "Yip" Harburg to satirize the gold reserve system in the United States, Harburg's flight of fancy took him to rainbows, pots of gold that could grant three wishes, and leprechauns. The story revolves around an Irish immigrant named Finian McLonergan, who buries a pot of gold in Rainbow Valley, Missitucky. He expects the gold to grow and make him rich. The stolen gold came from the leprechaun, Og. Bigoted southern senator Billboard Rawkins is taking land away from people who owe back taxes. Finian's daughter, Sharon, who is homesick for Ireland, is pursued by labor organizer Woody Mahoney, who is trying to raise the money for the taxes. Woody's sister, Susan, can't speak, so she dances to communicate. In the end, the lesson is that wealth is counted in the people we know and love, not in precious metal. There was a 1968 movie of the musical starring Fred Astaire, Petula Clark, and Tommy Steele.

The Authors

Music by Burton Lane; Lyrics by E.Y. "Yip" Harburg; Book by E.Y. "Yip" Harburg and Fred Saidy

New York Runs

January 10, 1947–October 2, 1948: 46th Street Theatre

May 18, 1955–May 29, 1955: New York City Center (starring Helen Gallagher and Merv Griffin)

May 23, 1960–June 1, 1960: 46th Street Theatre

April 5, 1967–April 23, 1967: New York City Center Light Opera

April 6, 2004–May 30, 2004: Irish Repertory Theatre (starring Melissa Errico and Malcolm Gets)

The Song

"Look to the Rainbow" CD 1 / TRACK 18

When Woody asks Sharon (played by Ella Logan in the original Broadway production and Petula Clark in the movie version) to tell him about herself, she replies by singing "Look to the Rainbow," a song that tells a Glocca Morra legend.

Song Type

standard Broadway/ballad

Suggested 16-Bar Cut for Auditions

m. 53 through m. 64 + m. 73 through m. 76

A Funny Thing Happened on the Way to the Forum

The Show

This show is based on characters found in the comic plays of Greek playwright Titus Maccius Plautus (254 BC–184 BC). It takes us through the comic adventures of the slave Pseudolus as he strives to obtain his freedom by assisting his young master, Hero, who is trying to woo the young virgin, Philia, who lives among the courtesans in a neighboring house. Philia has been promised to a military captain, Miles Gloriosus. Pseudolus's efforts to thwart their union so that Hero and Philia can be together—and so he can be free—make for a bawdy and hilarious evening filled with close calls and mistaken identities. A film version of this musical was made in 1966 starring Zero Mostel, Jack Gilford, Buster Keaton, Michael Crawford, and Phil Silvers.

The Authors

Music and Lyrics by Stephen Sondheim; Book by Burt Shevelove and Larry Gelbart

New York Runs

May 8, 1962–August 29, 1964: Alvin Theatre

March 30, 1972–August 12, 1972: Lunt-Fontanne Theatre

April 18, 1996–January 4, 1998: St. James Theatre

The Song

"That'll Show Him" CD 2 / TRACK 14

In "That'll Show Him," Philia, the young virgin who is the apple of Hero's eye, tells Hero that she will exact her revenge on being taken by the captain by thinking of Hero when she is making love to Miles Gloriosus. (Philia was played by Donna McKechnie in the first touring cast, by Preshy Marker in the first Broadway production, and by Annette Andre in the 1966 movie.)

Song Type

standard Broadway/uptempo

Suggested 16-Bar Cuts for Auditions

m. 42 through m. 55

m. 34 through m. 40 (playing m. 45 accompaniment under the word "there" still sung on C, which should be held for three counts, and then singing the pickup, "I'll," to m. 46) + m. 46 through m. 55

Gypsy

The Show

This backstage story of Gypsy Rose Lee centers around her ambitious mother, Mama Rose, whose sole purpose in life is to advance the career of her vaudevillian daughter, June. Once June elopes with a young dancer, Mama Rose focuses on June's older, less-talented sister, Louise. Louise eventually becomes a successful stripper—using the stage name "Gypsy Rose Lee"—in burlesque shows, and no longer needs her mother's representation. Mama Rose is left alone, having rejected the marriage proposal of the kind theatrical agent, Herbie, and being no longer needed by her daughters. A film was made of the show in 1962 starring Rosalind Russell, Natalie Wood, and Karl Malden. A 1993 TV movie starred Bette Midler as Mama Rose.

The Authors

Music by Jule Styne; Lyrics by Stephen Sondheim; Book by Arthur Laurents

New York Runs

May 21, 1959–March 25, 1961: Broadway Theatre

September 23, 1974–January 4, 1975: Winter Garden Theatre

November 16, 1989–July 28, 1991: St. James Theatre (11/16/89–1/6/91); Marquis Theatre (4/18/91–7/28/91)

May 1, 2003–May 30, 2004: Shubert Theatre

The Song

"Little Lamb" CD 1 / TRACK 17

It is Louise's birthday, and, as usual, Mama Rose is more interested in obtaining the next booking for Baby June than paying full attention to Louise. An ignored Louise sings "Little Lamb" to her birthday present, a baby lamb. (Louise was originally played by Sandra Church on Broadway and by Natalie Wood in the 1962 film.)

Song Type

standard Broadway/ballad

Suggested 16-Bar Cut for Auditions

m. 21 through m. 30 (singing "lamb" not "fish" in m. 29 and m. 30, and singing "I" instead of "do" in m. 30) + m. 35 through m. 40

Jacques Brel Is Alive and Well and Living in Paris

The Show

In this American musical revue, four actors, two male and two female, sing songs by the Belgian songwriter Jacques Brel. Brel was a perceptive observer of life and truly a poet. The songs were beautifully translated into English by Eric Blau and Brel's friend Mort Shuman, and maintain their European flavor through their musical settings, often accompanied by accordion in performance.

Brel's songs, which express the universal and timeless experiences of love, death, war, and loss, struck audiences of the late '60s and early '70s as the European counterparts of Bob Dylan's songs. A 1974 film starred Elly Stone, Mort Shuman, Joe Masiell, Paul Marchall, and Jacques Brel himself.

The Authors

Music, Lyrics, and Commentary by Jacques Brel; Additional Material by Mort Shuman and Eric Blau

New York Runs

January 22, 1968–July 2, 1972: Village Gate (Off-Broadway)

September 15, 1972–October 28, 1972: Royale Theatre

January 22, 1988–February 12,1988: The Town Hall (20th Anniversary Production)

1992 revival: Village Gate (Off-Broadway)

1974 revival: Astor Place Theatre (Off-Broadway)

March 27, 2006–February 25, 2007: The Zipper Theatre (Off-Broadway)

The Song

"I Loved (J'aimais)" CD 1 / TRACK 11

"I Loved" is a nostalgic song, filled with poetic images, that ends with a twist of irony.

Song Type

Difficult to categorize, this song could be used to audition for a revue or cabaret of French songs, perhaps for A. . . MY NAME IS ALICE, or for an Edith Piaf revue. It lies somewhere between an uptempo and a ballad, but could best be considered a ballad.

Suggested 16-Bar Cut for Auditions

m. 21 (with pickup if singing first verse) through m. 36

Li'l Abner

The Show

Based on the long-running syndicated comic strip, *Li'l Abner* takes place in rural Dogpatch, U.S.A., where sexy Daisy Mae Scragg persists in trying to get the good-looking simpleton, Abner Yokum, to marry her. Mammy Yokum concocted Yokumberry Tonic, an elixir that makes men strong and handsome but has the side effect of causing them to have no interest in sex. Mammy's son, Abner, has obviously partaken of this brew. There is a threat that Dogpatch might be turned into a nuclear testing site. But the town is saved from destruction when a plaque is discovered pronouncing local bungling Confederate general Jubilation T. Cornpone a hero of the Republic, because he was instrumental in the defeat of his own army. The biggest production number in the show takes place during the annual Sadie Hawkins' Day celebration. Sadie Hawkins was a plain young woman whose father came up with the idea of the event during which unmarried women of the town could pursue the available bachelors in a foot race. A 1959 movie of the musical starred Peter Palmer as Abner.

The Authors

Music by Gene de Paul; Lyrics by Johnny Mercer; Book by Norman Panama and Melvin Frank

New York Run

November 15, 1956–July 12, 1958: St. James Theatre

The Song

"Namely You" CD 2 / TRACK 7

Daisy Mae (played by Edie Adams [billed as "Edith Adams"] on Broadway and Leslie Parrish in the film) has been promised in an arranged marriage to the less-than-desirable Earthquake McGoon.

Abner promises Daisy Mae that he will let her catch him in the Sadie Hawkins Day race. He then tells her in the duet "Namely You" that she deserves better than McGoon. The version of the song in this book is Daisy Mae's portion of the duet.

Song Type
standard Broadway/ballad

Suggested 16-Bar Cut for Auditions
m. 19 through m. 35

Mamma Mia!

The Show
Based on the songs of the Swedish rock group ABBA, the title of this show is from their 1975 hit "Mamma Mia." The action takes place on a fictional Greek Island where Sophie Sheriden is preparing for her wedding. Her quest to discover who her real father is, so that he can give her away at the ceremony, brings three men from her mother's past—Harry "Head Banger" Bright, Bill Austin, and Sam Carmichael—back to the island they last visited 20 years ago. In addition, Donna, Sophie's mother, invites two old friends—Tanya and Rosie—with whom she used to have a singing group, to join her on the island. Mistaken identities and misunderstandings make for a fun time. Ultimately Sam and Donna get married and Sophie does not.

The Authors
Music and Lyrics by Benny Andersson and Björn Ulvaeus; Book by Catherine Johnson

New York Runs
October 18, 2001–present: Winter Garden Theatre (10/18/01–5/4/02); Cadillac Winter Garden Theatre (5/5/02–12/31/06); Winter Garden Theatre (1/1/07–present)

The Songs

"Mamma Mia" * CD 2 / TRACK 3
"Mamma Mia" is sung by Donna Sheriden (Louise Pitre originated the role on Broadway) when she is surprised by the arrival of three men from her past, one of whom Sophie thinks might be her father. In this song, Donna recalls her

former relationships with each of the three men. [This was the last song written for the *ABBA* album, but ended up being its opening track. When he wrote the lyrics for this song, Björn had in mind the image of a woman confronting a man.]

Song Type
pop rock/uptempo

Suggested 16-Bar Cut for Auditions
m. 23 through m. 38 + m. 58 through m. 59

"The Name of the Game" * CD 2 / TRACK 6
"The Name of the Game" is sung by Sophie (played by Tina Maddigan on Broadway), with Bill Austin, as she asks him if he feels the same way she does. By the end of the song, Sophie has three fathers to give her away. Her mother then informs Sophie that she will give her away instead. [Set to music Benny and Björn had already written, the lyric for this song was originally written by Björn for Lasse Hallström who was directing *ABBA: The Movie*. In the movie, a reporter was chasing ABBA around during their Australian tour trying to get an interview with them. There is a short sequence in the film in which he dreams that he is a therapist, and Agnetha, a member of ABBA, is lying on the couch pouring out her emotions to him.]

Song Type
pop rock/uptempo

Suggested 16-Bar Cuts for Auditions
m. 19 through m. 34

m. 60 (with the pickup) through m. 73 (This cut shows lower notes in the vocal range.)

"The Winner Takes It All" CD 2 / TRACK 17
Donna sings "The Winner Takes It All" as she confronts Sam, doing her best to hide the feelings she has always had for him. [Some think that this song has to do with Björn's divorce from Agnetha, but he denies this, saying that it does not apply to them because there was no winner in their case.]

Song Type
pop rock/ballad

Suggested 16-Bar Cut for Auditions
m. 36 through m. 54

*Stig Anderson also contributed to the lyrics for these songs.

A Man of No Importance

The Show

Based on the 1994 film of the same name, this show tells the story of a bus driver named Alfie Byrne who lives and works in Dublin in the 1960s. A huge fan of Oscar Wilde, Alfie wants to stage a version of *Salome* in his small parish church, St. Imelda's. The church authorities are against this idea but Alfie fights to make it happen. In the process he comes to terms with his own sexuality.

The Authors

Music by Stephen Flaherty; Lyrics by Lynn Ahrens; Book by Terrence McNally

New York Run

September 12, 2002–December 29, 2002: Lincoln Center Theater (Off-Broadway)

The Songs

"Princess" CD 2 / TRACK 8

Adele Rice (originally played by Sally Murphy) first met Alfie as a passenger on his bus. Though Adele insists that she is not an actress, Alfie tries to persuade her to play the part of Princess Salome in his theatrical production. In the song "Princess," Adele tells Alfie that the small-town life she left behind makes her anything but a "princess."

Song Type

contemporary musical theatre/uptempo

Suggested 16-Bar Cuts for Auditions

m. 54 through m. 68

m. 46 through m. 66 + m. 68

"Love Who You Love" (reprise)
CD 2 / TRACK 2

"Love Who You Love" (reprise) is sung by Adele, single and pregnant, as she sets off for London to make a life for her child. She sings this song to Alfie who has also had his secret disclosed to the world—that he is a gay man. As Adele turns Alfie's words back on him, we see that Adele and Alfie have helped each other learn that there is no shame in love.

Song Type

contemporary musical theatre/ballad

Suggested 16-Bar Cut for Auditions

m. 67 (with pickup) through m. 88 + m. 91

My Fair Lady

The Show

Based on the well-known George Bernard Shaw play *Pygmalion*, the musical remains true to the intents of the original story, which purported that there are no true class distinctions in society, only differences in levels of education. Cockney Eliza Doolittle is taken on as a student by linguist Henry Higgins, who has wagered with his colleague, Colonel Pickering, that he can transform her into a lady. Higgins succeeds in neutralizing her accent to the extent that Eliza begins to move well in higher society. A young upper-class man, Freddy Eynsford-Hill, falls in love with Eliza, as does Professor Higgins. We are left not knowing who eventually wins her affections. A film version was released in 1964 starring Audrey Hepburn and Rex Harrison.

The Authors

Music by Frederick Loewe; Lyrics and Book by Alan Jay Lerner

New York Runs

March 15, 1956–September 29, 1962: Mark Hellinger Theatre

March 25, 1976–February 20, 1977: St. James Theatre (3/25/76–12/5/76); Lunt-Fontanne Theatre (12/9/76–2/20/77)

August 18, 1981–November 29, 1981: Uris Theatre

December 9, 1993–May 1, 1994: Virginia Theatre

The Songs

"I Could Have Danced All Night"
CD 1 / TRACK 10

"I Could Have Danced All Night" is sung by Eliza (played by Julie Andrews on Broadway and Audrey Hepburn [whose singing was dubbed by Marni Nixon] in the movie) as she anticipates the challenge of an upper-class social event for which Prof. Higgins feels she is ready.

Song Type

standard Broadway/legit musical theatre/uptempo

Suggested 16-Bar Cut for Auditions

m. 30 (with pickups) through m. 42 + m. 92 (Coda) through m. 96

"Show Me" CD 2 / TRACK 9

"Show Me" is sung by Eliza when she runs into Freddy, who spends many a night outside her home, as she leaves after become infuriated at Higgins's and Pickering's self-congratulations regarding her accomplishments. Freddy ardently tries to express his feelings to her but takes out her fury on him.

Song Type

standard Broadway/legit musical theatre/uptempo

Suggested 16-Bar Cut for Auditions

m. 57 through m. 68 + m. 73 through m. 76 (using first verse lyrics)

"Without You" CD 2 / TRACK 18

Eliza sings "Without You" to Henry Higgins when he comes to retrieve her from his mother's home where she has gone to seek advice. After expressing her feelings through this song, Eliza tells Higgins that he will never see her again and she walks out.

Song Type

standard Broadway/legit musical theatre/uptempo

Suggested 16-Bar Cut for Auditions

m. 50 (with pickup) through m. 65

Oh, Kay!

The Show

In the fictional town of Beachampton, Long Island, a band of bootleggers have set up their headquarters in an empty beach house. When the owner of the house, Jimmy Winter, returns home unexpectedly, Kay Denham (who is really Lady Kay Rutfield) poses as a member of the house staff in order to be near the bootlegged liquor that her highborn, but shady, brother, The Duke, has stored in Jimmy's basement. Though Jimmy is engaged to someone else, he eventually falls in love with Kay and she returns his feelings. Mistaken identities and other comic confusions eventually resolve to keep Kay and Jimmy together. A 1928 silent(!) movie was the only film version made of the musical.

The Authors

Music by George Gershwin; Lyrics by Ira Gershwin; Book by Guy Bolton and P. G. Wodehouse

New York Runs

November 8, 1926–June 1927: Imperial Theatre

January, 1928, for 16 performances: Century Theatre

November 1, 1990–April 14, 1991: Richard Rodgers Theatre (11/1/90–1/5/91); Lunt-Fontanne Theatre (4/2/91–4/14/91) (This was an all-Black version of the show starring Brian Stokes Mitchell as Jimmy.)

The Song

"Someone to Watch Over Me" CD 2 / TRACK 12

In "Someone to Watch Over Me," Kay (originally played by Gertrude Lawrence—her first starring role on Broadway) longs for protective warmth in her life.

Song Type

standard Broadway/ballad

Suggested 16-Bar Cut for Auditions

m. 44 through m. 60

Once on This Island

The Show

Set in the French Antilles, this show is based on the novel *My Love, My Love* by Rosa Guy, which is a retelling of Hans Christian Andersen's *The Little Mermaid*. Ti Moune, a peasant girl, asks the gods—Erzulie (the god of Love), Asaka (the god of Earth), Agwe (the god of Water), and Papa Ge (the god of Death)—to help her meet an upper-class boy (Grande Homme) named Daniel. Agwe causes Daniel to have an automobile accident, and Ti Moune takes care of him until he is fully recovered. The two fall in love. The strength of Ti Moune's love is then tested by the gods as they send her on an eventful journey. She eventually learns that Daniel is engaged to someone else, whom he finally marries. Ultimately, Ti Moune dies, steadfast in her love for Daniel, and she is reincarnated as a tree, which cracks open the wall of the hotel where Daniel's family lives. We then see a peasant girl and Daniel's son playing in the tree. *Once on This Island* shows the ways in which people use stories to understand their own experiences and come to terms with loss.

The Authors

Music by Stephen Flaherty; Lyrics and Book by Lynn Ahrens

New York Run

October 18, 1990–December 1, 1991: Booth Theatre

The Songs

"Waiting for Life"   CD 2 / TRACK 15

"Waiting for Life" is the song in which Ti Moune (originally played by LaChanze) catches sight of an upper-class boy (Daniel, a Grande Homme) and asks the gods to set her fate in motion at last.

Song Type

contemporary musical theatre/uptempo

Suggested 16-Bar Cut for Auditions

m. 119 (with pickup) through m. 129 +
m. 134 through m. 141

"The Human Heart"   CD 1 / TRACK 8

"The Human Heart" is sung by Erzulie, Goddess of Love (originally played by Andrea Frierson), who blesses Ti Moune for having the courage to follow her heart across the island to Daniel. According to the composer, "The song… is as much about community as it is about romantic love."

Song Type

contemporary musical theatre/uptempo

Suggested 16-Bar Cut for Auditions

m. 32 (with pickup) through m. 45

Pal Joey

The Show

Based on John O'Hara's series of short stories in *The New Yorker*, this musical is about Joey Evans, a second-rate dancing entertainer in 1930s Chicago. Joey drops his girlfriend, Linda English, to become wealthy Vera Simpson's gigolo, hoping to persuade her to set him up in his own club. Simpson, who is married, falls victim to a blackmail attempt, but Linda thwarts it. Ultimately, Joey is dropped by Vera and rejected by Linda. A movie version in 1957 starred Frank Sinatra, Rita Hayworth, and Kim Novak.

The Authors

Music by Richard Rodgers; Lyrics by Lorenz Hart; Book by John O'Hara (uncredited: George Abbott)

New York Runs

December 25, 1940–November 29, 1941: Ethel Barrymore Theatre (12/25/40–8/16/41); Shubert Theatre (9/1/41–10/21/41); St. James Theatre (10/21/41–11/29/41)

January 3, 1952–April 18, 1953: Broadhurst Theatre

May 29, 1963–June 9, 1963: City Center

June 27, 1976–August 29, 1976: Circle in the Square Theatre

May 4, 1995–May 6, 1995: City Center (concert version)

The Songs

"What Is a Man?"   CD 2 / TRACK 16

Though Joey was instructed by the club owner to keep patron Vera Simpson (played by Leila Ernst on Broadway, Rita Hayworth [singing dubbed by Jo Ann Greer] in the movie, and Patti LuPone in the 1995 concert version) happy, he ends up insulting her and she walks out. The next day, she phones him, and he bawls her out for getting him fired. Vera finds his directness attractive and sings "What Is a Man?" while alone in her boudoir.

Song Type

standard Broadway/ballad (with a short uptempo section in the middle)

Suggested 16-Bar Cut for Auditions
m. 27 through m. 46

"Bewitched, Bothered and Bewildered"
CD 1 / TRACK 1

"Bewitched, Bothered and Bewildered" is sung by Vera after outfitting Joey in a new suit of clothes at a swanky tailor's shop. She has been totally charmed by the brash and impudent Joey, and is ready to pamper him.

Song Type

standard Broadway/ballad

Suggested 16-Bar Cut for Auditions
m. 37 through 50 + m. 53 through m. 54
(If using first verse lyrics, sing "me" on the last note.)

Passion

The Show

An Italian army captain, Giorgio, is assigned to a remote outpost. The emotionally and physically unwell Fosca, cousin of his direct superor Colonel Ricci, lives there, and, for the most part, confines herself to her room reading. Giorgio is kind to her, lending her books and trying to get her to appreciate the good and beautiful things around her. Fosca, who is unattractive and lonely, wants Giorgio to be more than her friend. Giorgio is in love with Clara, his married mistress, whom he has had to leave behind. Fosca becomes obsessed with Giorgio, to the extent of trying to prevent his leaving on a brief trip. Giorgio goes to visit Clara and writes Fosca, explaining that he is in love with someone else. When Giorgio returns to the outpost, Fosca has become more ill. Colonel Ricci then explains to Giorgio that Fosca had been deceived and defrauded by her husband, and that this had destroyed her emotionally. Fosca continues to be obsessed with Giorgio, and he begins to feel responsible towards her, complicating and eventually ending his relationship with Clara. Ultimately, Fosca dies believing that she was truly loved, and Giorgio is left ill and alone.

The Authors

Music by and Lyrics by Stephen Sondheim; Book by James Lapine

New York Runs

May 9, 1994–January 7, 1995: Plymouth Theatre

October 20, 2004: Ambassador Theatre (special benefit concert)

The Song

"Forty Days"   CD 1 / TRACK 4

"Forty Days" is sung by Clara (played by Marin Mazzie on Broadway) as she prepares for what she hopes will be an extended visit from Giorgio, while he is on sick leave and her husband is out of town.

Song Type

standard Broadway/uptempo

Suggested 16-Bar Cut for Auditions
m. 20 through m. 36

Porgy and Bess®

The Show

Considered an opera historically, *Porgy and Bess* was based on DuBose Heyward's 1925 novel, *Porgy*. It is the story of the crippled beggar Porgy, a dock worker named Crown, Crown's woman Bess, and a drug dealer named Sportin' Life. The action takes place in the Catfish Row section of Charleston, South Carolina. The show involves a craps game, a murder, Crown running out on Bess, Porgy sheltering Bess, Sportin' Life's courting of Bess, her refusal, Crown's return, Clara's and Jake's deaths in a storm, Porgy's murder of Crown, Porgy's arrest, Bess's eventual submission to Sportin' Life, and Porgy's final pursuit of Bess. A 1959 screen version of the musical starred Sidney Poitier, Dorothy Dandridge, and Sammy Davis, Jr.

The Authors

Music by George Gershwin; Lyrics by DuBose Heyward and Ira Gershwin; Book by DuBose Heyward

New York Runs

October 10, 1935–January 25, 1936:
Alvin Theatre

January 22, 1942–September 26, 1942:
Majestic Theatre

September 13, 1943–October 2, 1943:
44th Street Theatre

March 10,1953–November 28, 1953:
Ziegfeld Theatre

September 25, 1976–January 9, 1977:
Uris Theatre (9/25/76–12/5/76);
Mark Hellinger Theatre (12/7/76–1/9/77)

April 7, 1983–May 15, 1983: Radio City
Music Hall

The Songs

"Summertime" CD 2 / TRACK 13

"Summertime" is sung near the beginning of
the show by a fisherman's wife, Clara (played in
the original production by Abbie Mitchell), as a
lullaby to their baby.

Song Type

standard Broadway/ballad

Suggested 16-Bar Cut for Auditions

m. 8 (with pickups) through m. 24

"Leavin' for the Promise' Lan'"
CD 1 / TRACK 16

A game of craps that was organized by Porgy
leaves two final players, Crown and Robbins,
who have become very inebriated. After Robbins
wins, a fight ensues between Crown and him and
Robbins ends up dead. "Leavin' for the Promise'
Lan'" is sung by Bess and the Ensemble at the
end of Act I, after the undertaker has agreed to
bury Robbins so long as his wife, Serena, pays the
undertaker back. The ensemble vocals have been
removed from this number for the purposes of this
book, leaving Bess's solo intact.

Song Type

standard Broadway/legit musical theatre/uptempo

Suggested 16-Bar Cut for Auditions

m. 72 (with pickups) through m. 87

The Secret Garden

The Show

This show is based on the Frances Hodgson
Burnett book of the same name. Mary Lennox,
a young, spoiled rich girl, is forced to move to
England to live with her Uncle Archibald after
her parents dies in a cholera epidemic in India.
Archibald is grieving over the loss of his wife, who
died giving birth to their crippled son, Colin, who
is now kept isolated in his room. Mary reminds
Archibald of his deceased wife, Lily, and this
resemblance makes it difficult for him to relate
to her. Mary, meanwhile, befriends the chamber
maid, Martha, and Dickon, the son of the gardener.
Mary discovers a walled garden that is unkempt
and overgrown. While Archibald is away on a
much-needed trip, she and Dickon bring Colin to
the garden, where he begins to thrive on the fresh
air and exercise. When Archibald returns, Colin is
up and about, and Archibald finally accepts Mary
as part of the family.

The Authors

Music by Lucy Simon; Lyrics and Book by Marsha
Norman

New York Run

April 25, 1991–January 3, 1993: St. James Theatre

The Songs

"Come to My Garden" CD 1 / TRACK 2

"Come to My Garden" is sung by Lily's ghost
(played by Rebecca Luker on Broadway) and
her son, Colin, when he has been brought to the
garden for the first time. The version of the song
in this book is Lily's solo portion of the duet.

Song Type

standard Broadway/ballad

Suggested 16-Bar Cut for Auditions

m. 13 through m. 31

"How Could I Ever Know?" CD 1 / TRACK 7

"How Could I Ever Know?" is sung by Lily's
ghost to convince Archibald that he should end his
trip and go home.

Song Type

standard Broadway/ballad

Suggested 16-Bar Cuts for Auditions
m. 24 (with pickup) through m. 45
m. 32 through m. 45

Strike Up the Band

The Show

In this satirical anti-war musical, political sentiments are expressed comedically. The owner of the Fletcher American Cheese Co., Horace J. Fletcher, is outraged when Switzerland protests the tariff imposed by the U.S. President on imported cheese. He convinces the U.S. government to declare a war, which he will finance and call "The Horace J. Fletcher Memorial War." When his daughter, Joan, reveals her love for Jim Townsend, a reporter who has publicly criticized both the war and the quality of milk going into his cheese, Fletcher drafts him and sends him off to fight. Everything ends in patriotic exultation with the lovers reunited, Townsend a hero, and a new war brewing with Russia over a tariff on caviar.

Note: This show failed to make it to Broadway in 1927 and was rewritten to take place in a chocolate factory for the 1930 production. The 1927 version of the show is the one currently available for rental.

The Authors

Music by George Gershwin; Lyrics by Ira Gershwin; Book by George S. Kaufman

New York Run

January 14, 1930–June 28, 1930: Times Square Theatre

The Songs

"The Man I Love" CD 2 / TRACK 4

Jim is reluctant to go off to a war that is about cheese; in fact, he doesn't even like cheese. Joan (played on Broadway by Margaret Shilling) tells him that the man she loves would have no reservations about fighting for something that matters to her. She sings "The Man I Love" and Jim joins her with his feelings about "the girl I love." The version of the song in this book is derived from the female portion of the duet.

Song Type
standard Broadway/ballad

Suggested 16-Bar Cut for Auditions
m. 37 through m. 53

"Hangin' Around with You" CD 1 / TRACK 6

"Hangin' Around with You" is sung by Anne (played on Broadway by Doris Carson), the daughter of society do-gooder Mrs. Draper who has tried to enlist Horace Fletcher's help with one of her projects, and Timothy, the foreman of the cheese factory with whom Anne is in love. Anne wants to marry Timothy before he goes off to battle. Not in the 1927 show, this song was written specifically for the 1930 production, but is available for optional inclusion in the show as a replacement for "Yankee Doodle Rhythm."

Song Type
standard Broadway/uptempo

Suggested 16-Bar Cut for Auditions
m. 38 through m. 54

Sweeney Todd

The Show

Taking place in London during the Industrial Revolution, this show is based on Christopher Bond's 1973 play *Sweeney Todd*, which is a version of the story told in the 1847 British play by George Dibdin Pitt titled *The String of Pearls, or The Fiend of Fleet Street*. It is the story of a barber who escapes from a prison where he was sent after being wrongly convicted of a crime. He returns to take out his revenge on the judge who sentenced him. The judge had subsequently raped Todd's wife and had plans to marry Todd's daughter. Sweeney becomes a serial killer, using his barber's razor to slit the throats of his victims. His accomplice, the baker Mrs. Lovett, then bakes the corpses into meat pies, which she sells in her shop. As far as romantic pairings are concerned, Mrs. Lovett is attracted to Todd, and the young sailor, Anthony, longs for Johanna. A taped performance of the touring company starring George Hearn and Angela Lansbury was shown on television in 1982. A San Francisco concert version starring George Hearn and Patti LuPone was broadcast on PBS in 2001. A film version, directed by Tim Burton and starring Johnny Depp and Helena Bonham Carter, was released in 2008.

The Authors

Music and Lyrics by Stephen Sondheim; Book by Hugh Wheeler

New York Runs

March 1, 1979–June 29, 1980: Uris Theatre (currently the Gershwin)

October 11, 1984–November 18, 1984: New York City Opera (13 performances)

September 14, 1989–February 25, 1990: Circle in the Square Theatre

November 3, 2005–September 3, 2006: Eugene O'Neill Theatre

The Song

"Green Finch and Linnet Bird"
CD 1 / TRACK 5

"Green Finch and Linnet Bird" is sung by Johanna (originally played by Sara Rice) as she gazes upon a bird seller's wares from the window of Judge Turpin's home. She feels imprisoned there and wonders why the caged birds still sing. It is during this song that Anthony sees Johanna for the first time and is attracted to her beauty.

Song Type

standard Broadway/uptempo

Suggested 16-Bar Cuts for Auditions

m. 23 through m. 38 + m. 61 through m. 65

m. 39 through m. 56 + m. 61 through m. 65

The Songs

LOVE, DON'T TURN AWAY

(from "110 in the Shade")

Words by
TOM JONES

Music by
HARVEY SCHMIDT

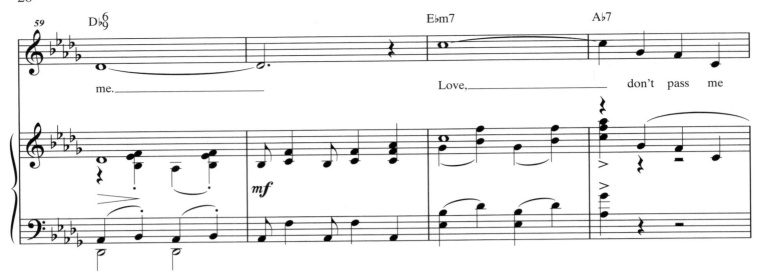

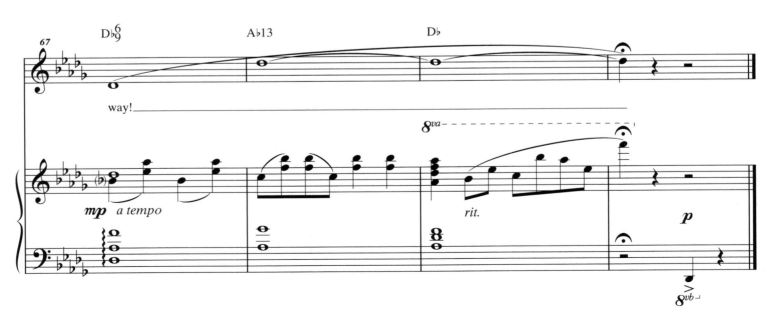

SIMPLE LITTLE THINGS

(from "110 in the Shade")

Words by
TOM JONES

Music by
HARVEY SCHMIDT

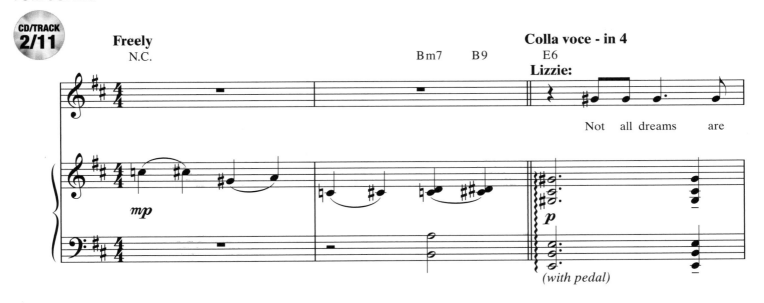

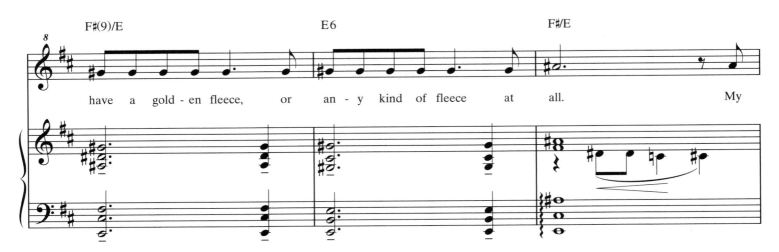

IS IT REALLY ME?

(from "110 in the Shade")

Words by
TOM JONES

Music by
HARVEY SCHMIDT

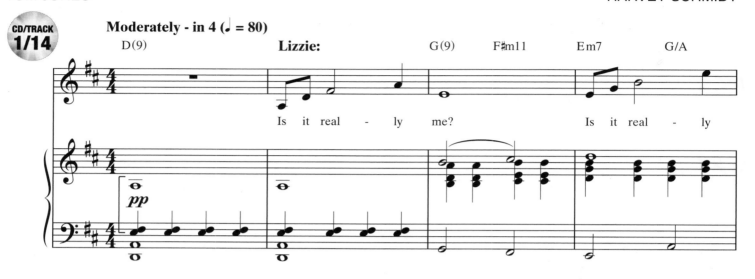

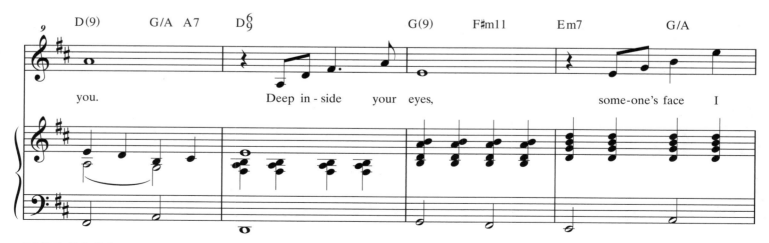

Is It Really Me? - 3 - 1
32766

THE LADY IS A TRAMP

(from "Babes in Arms")

Words by
LORENZ HART

Music by
RICHARD RODGERS

36

38

The Lady Is a Tramp - 5 - 4
32766

The Lady Is a Tramp - 5 - 5
32766

I CAN'T DO THE SUM

(from "Babes in Toyland")

Words by
GLEN MAC DONOUGH

Music by
VICTOR HERBERT

Moderato (♩ = 92)

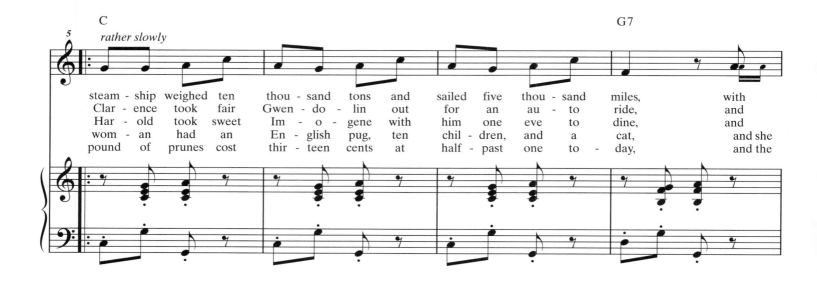

steam - ship weighed ten thou - sand tons and sailed five thou - sand miles, with
Clar - ence took fair Gwen - do - lin out for an au - to ride, and
Har - old took sweet Im - o - gene with him one eve to dine, and
wom - an had an En - glish pug, ten chil - dren, and a cat, and she

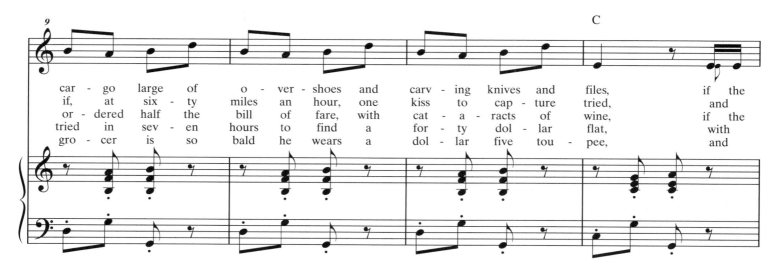

car - go large of o - ver - shoes and carv - ing knives and files, if the
if, at six - ty miles an hour, one kiss to cap - ture tried, and
or - dered half the bill of fare, with cat - a - racts of wine, if the
tried in sev - en hours to find a for - ty dol - lar flat, with
gro - cer is so bald he wears a dol - lar five tou - pee, and

I Can't Do The Sum - 3 - 1
32766

mates were al - most six feet high, and the bos' - n near the same, would
quite for - got the steer - ing gear, on her hon - eyed lips to sup, how
bill of fare were thir-teen nine-ty-five, and poor Har - old had but four, how
naught but sun - ny out - side rooms in a neigh - bor - hood of tone, how
if with ev - 'ry pound of tea he will give two cut - glass plates, how

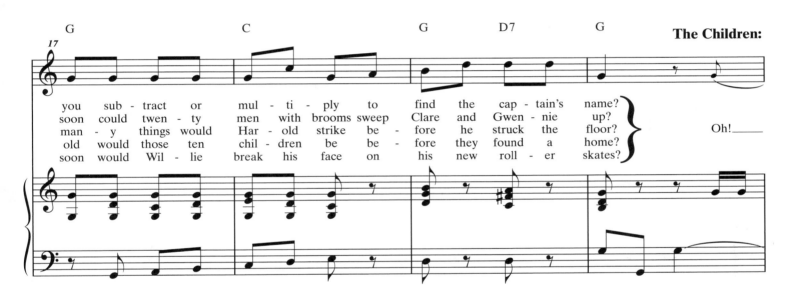

The Children:

you sub - tract or mul - ti - ply to find the cap - tain's name?
soon could twen - ty men with brooms sweep Clare and Gwen - nie up?
man - y things would Har - old strike be - fore he struck the floor?
old would those ten chil - dren be be - fore they found a home?
soon would Wil - lie break his face on his new roll - er skates?

Oh!_____

Oh!_____ Oh!_____

FALLING IN LOVE WITH LOVE

(from "The Boys From Syracuse")

Words by
LORENZ HART

Music by
RICHARD RODGERS

THE SIMPLE JOYS OF MAIDENHOOD

(from "Camelot")

Lyrics by
ALAN JAY LERNER

Music by
FREDERICK LOEWE

Shan't I, St. Genevieve? Why must I suffer this squalid destiny Just when I reach the

golden age of eligibility and wooability. Is my fate determined by love and courtship?

Oh, no. Clause one: fix the border; Clause two: establish trade;

Clause three: deliver me; Clause four: stop the war; five, six: pick up sticks. How cruel! How unjust!

Poco meno mosso

Am I never to know the joys of maidenhood? The conventional, ordinary, garden variety joys of maidenhood?

I LOVED YOU ONCE IN SILENCE

(from "Camelot")

Lyrics by
ALAN JAY LERNER

Music by
FREDERICK LOEWE

62

Lancelot: Jenny, it's because we're here, here in Camelot...
(Dialogue continues)

poco rubato

Optional (continuation of Scene)

Guenevere: ...What sort of heartbreaking solution is that?
Lancelot: Forgive me, Jenny, *(The music begins.)*

L'istesso tempo

I shall never mention it again, I swear.

Nor shall I come to see you again. I swear that too.

Guenevere: Lance? (He stops.) Have we no more tender words to say to each

other?

(She sings)

The si - lence_____ at last was bro - ken!

Mordred and Knights
tiptoe silently into the room.

We flung wide our pris-on door. Ev-'ry

joy-ous word of love was spo-ken... And af-ter

Andante (♩ = 100)

all had been said, here we are, my love, si-lent once more and not far, my love...

(Lancelot and Guenevere embrace.) Mordred: ...Lancelot, don't touch your dagger. (Lancelot whirls around.)

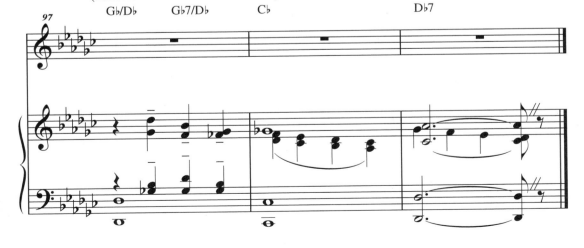

I accuse you of treason, and
order you both to stand trial
for your crime. Surrender in the
name of the King.
(Lancelot snatches the
sword from Mordred.)

MUCH MORE

(from "The Fantasticks")

Words by
TOM JONES

Music by
HARVEY SCHMIDT

Con moto (♩ = 120)

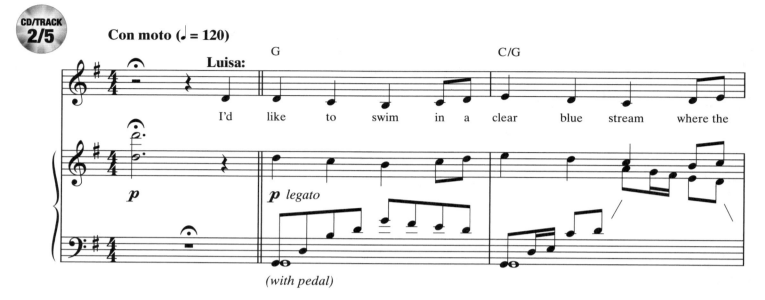

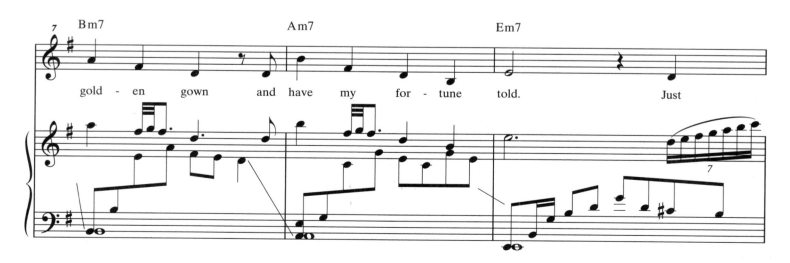

Much More - 5 - 1
32766

LOOK TO THE RAINBOW

(from "Finian's Rainbow")

Lyrics by
E. Y. HARBURG

Music by
BURTON LANE

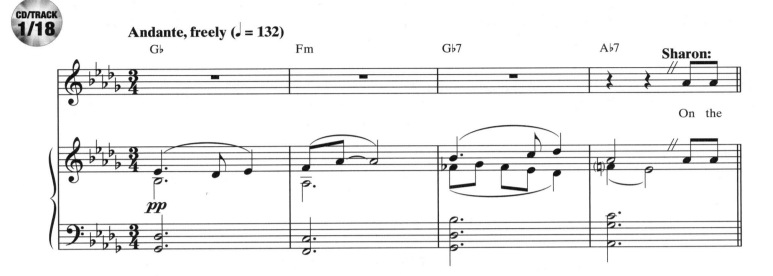

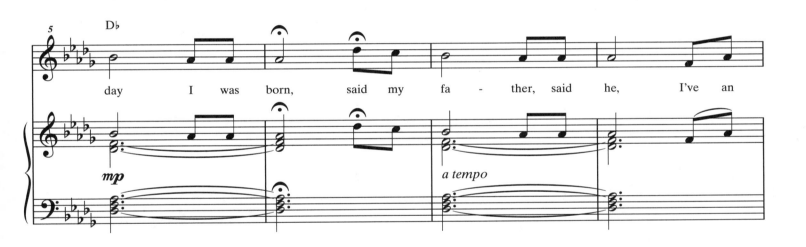

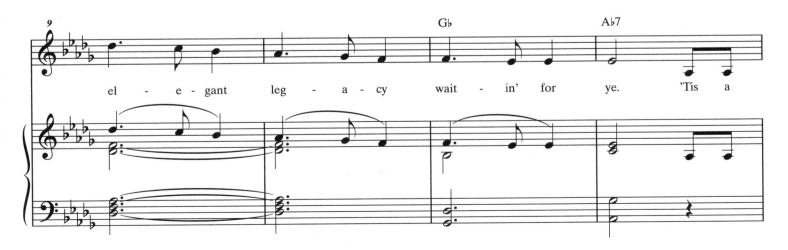

Look to the Rainbow - 5 - 1
32766

THAT'LL SHOW HIM

(from "A Funny Thing Happened on the Way to the Forum")

Music and Lyrics by
STEPHEN SONDHEIM

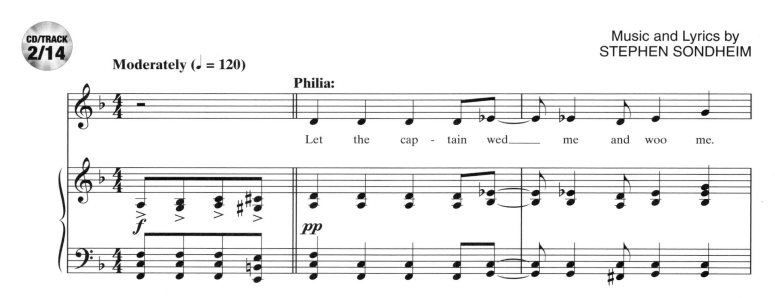

Philia:

Let the cap-tain wed____ me and woo me.

I shall play my part!____ Let him make his mad____ pas-sion to me.

You will have my heart.____ He can have the bod - y he paid for,

That'll Show Him - 4 - 1
32766

LITTLE LAMB

(from "Gypsy")

Lyrics by
STEPHEN SONDHEIM

Music by
JULE STYNE

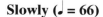

Little Lamb - 3 - 1
32766

I LOVED

(J'aimais)

(from "Jacques Brel Is Alive and Well and Living in Paris")

French Lyrics by
JACQUES BREL
English Lyrics by
MORT SHUMAN and ERIC BLAU

Music by
GERARD JOUANNEST
and FRANCOIS ROUBERT

NAMELY YOU
(from "Li'l Abner")

Words by
JOHNNY MERCER

Music by
GENE DE PAUL

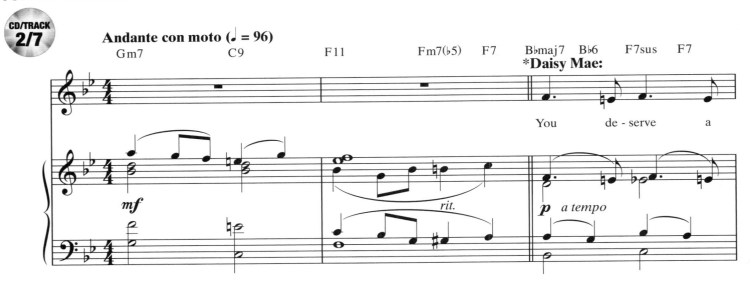

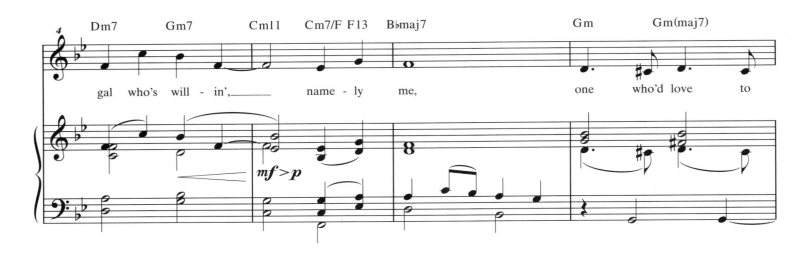

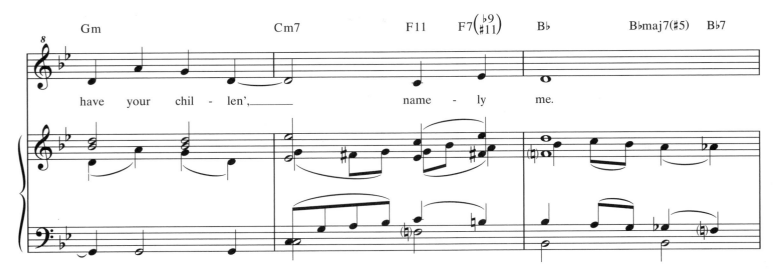

*Daisy Mae's solo has been excerpted from the original song.

Namely You - 3 - 1
32766

THE NAME OF THE GAME

(from "Mamma Mia!")

Words and Music by
BENNY ANDERSSON, STIG ANDERSON
and BJÖRN ULVAEUS

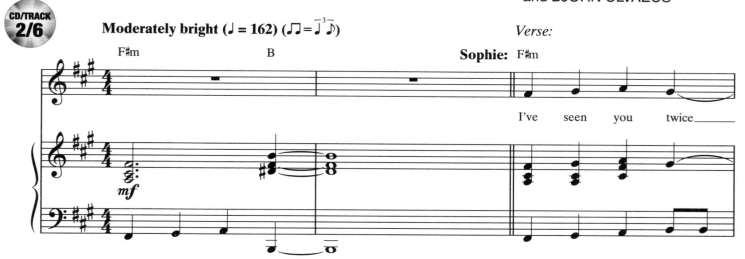

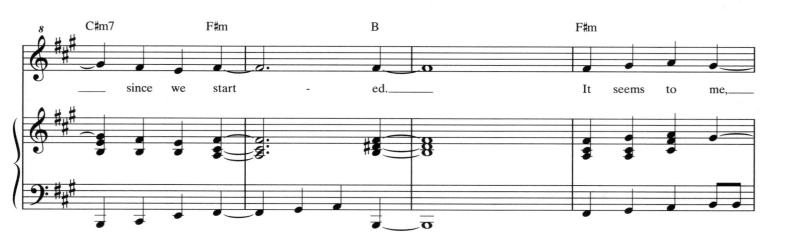

The Name of the Game - 7 - 1
32766

MAMMA MIA
(from "Mamma Mia!")

Words and Music by
BENNY ANDERSSON, STIG ANDERSON
and BJÖRN ULVAEUS

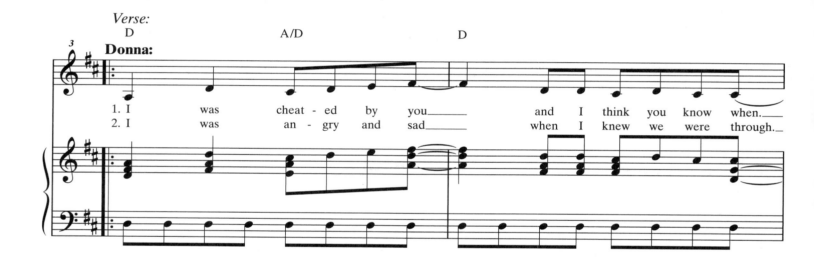

1. I was cheat-ed by you____ and I think you know when.____
2. I was an-gry and sad____ when I knew we were through.____

Mamma Mia - 6 - 1
32766

should not have let you go.

should not have let you go.

Donna: *What the hell are you all doing here? Well, I'd love to stop and chat, but I have to go and clean out my handbag or something.*

Bill: *Age does not wither her.*

Harry: *I was expecting a rather stout matron.*

THE WINNER TAKES IT ALL

(from "Mamma Mia!")

Words and Music by
BENNY ANDERSSON
and BJÖRN ULVAEUS

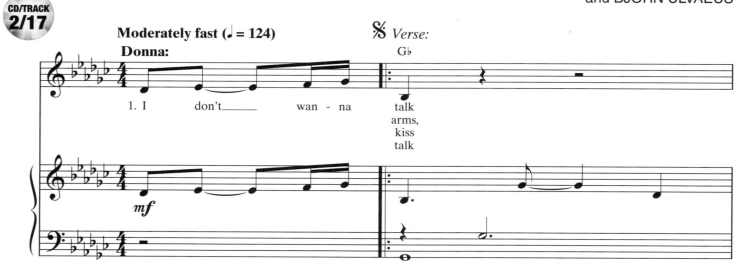

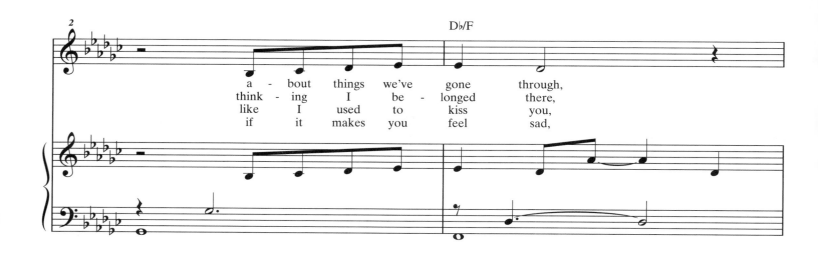

The Winner Takes It All - 7 - 1
32766

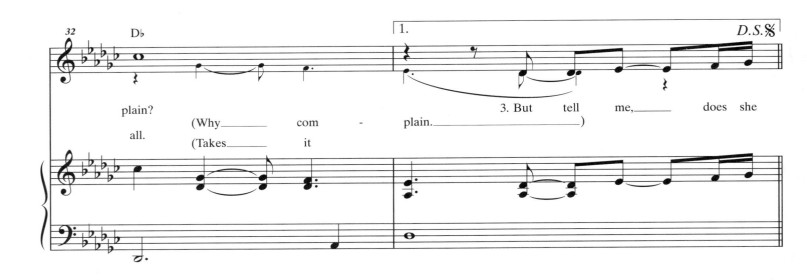

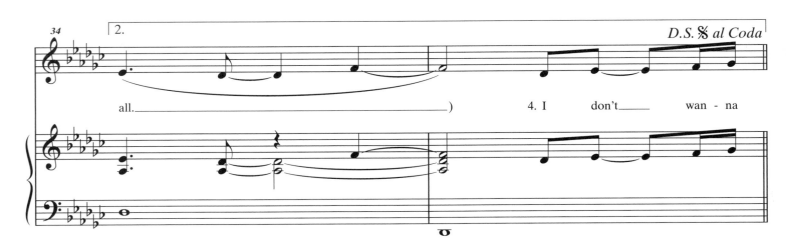

LOVE WHO YOU LOVE (REPRISE)
(from "A Man of No Importance")

Lyrics by
LYNN AHRENS

Music by
STEPHEN FLAHERTY

* At the composer's request, we have created a female version of the original song sung by the character Alfie.

Love Who You Love (Reprise) - 5 - 1
32766

PRINCESS
(from "A Man of No Importance")

Lyrics by
LYNN AHRENS

Music by
STEPHEN FLAHERTY

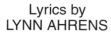

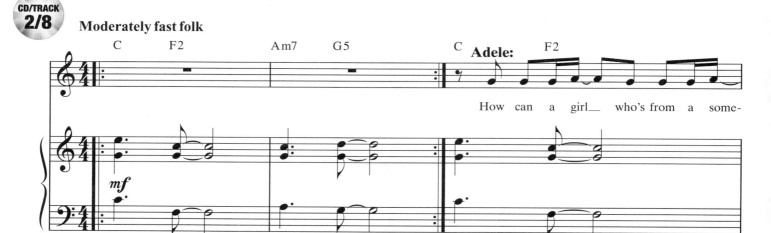

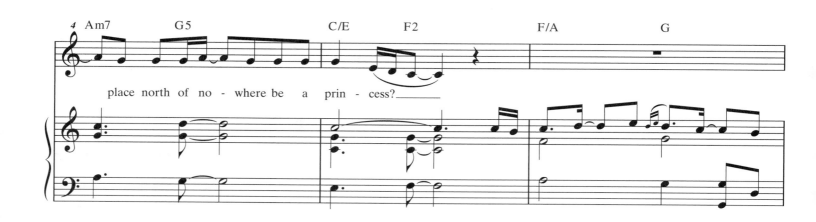

Princess - 6 - 1
32766

I COULD HAVE DANCED ALL NIGHT

(from "My Fair Lady")

Lyrics by
ALAN JAY LERNER

Music by
FREDERICK LOEWE

Allegro (♩ = 168)

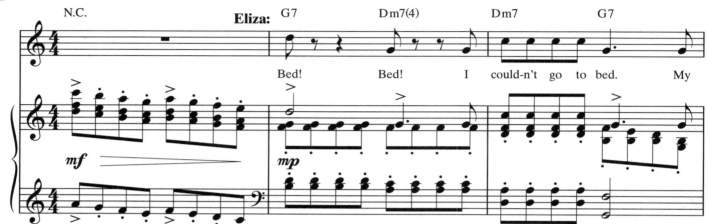

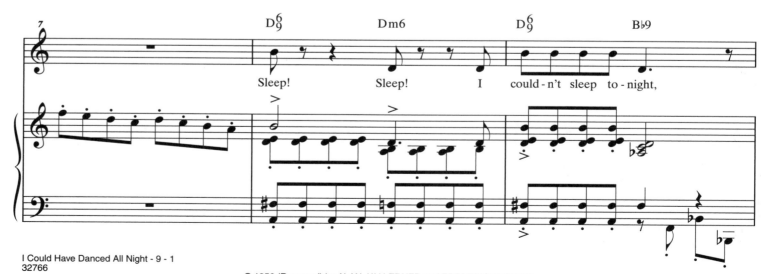

I Could Have Danced All Night - 9 - 1
32766

SHOW ME
(from "My Fair Lady")

Lyrics by
ALAN JAY LERNER

Music by
FREDERICK LOEWE

Subito agitato (♩ = 126)

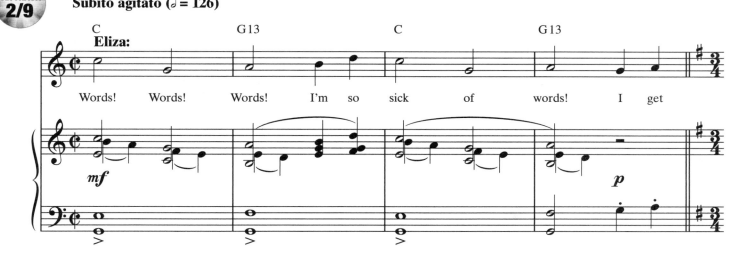

Eliza: Words! Words! Words! I'm so sick of words! I get

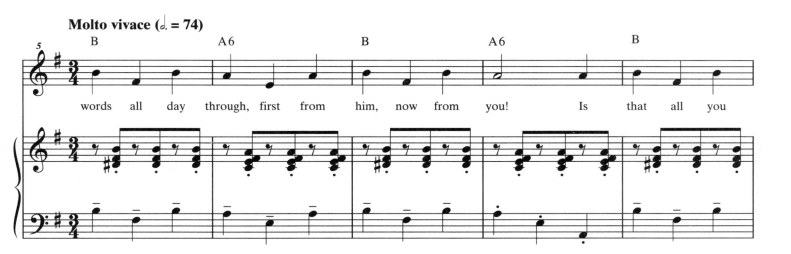

words all day through, first from him, now from you! Is that all you

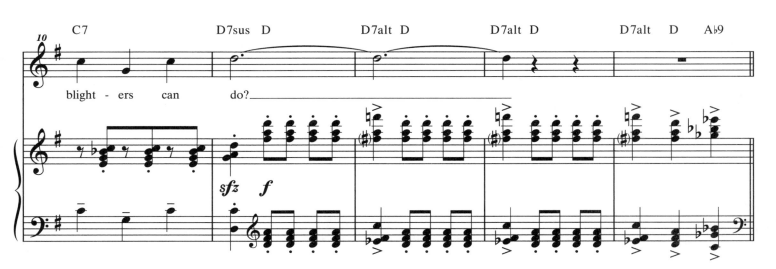

blight-ers can do?

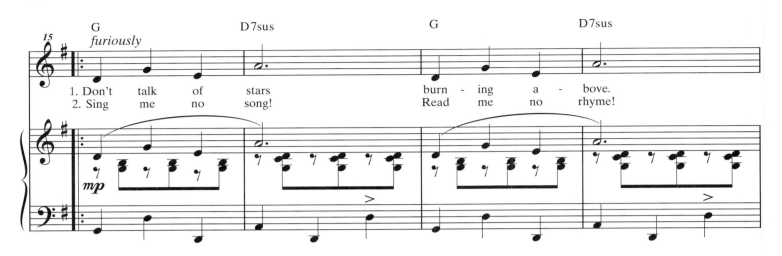

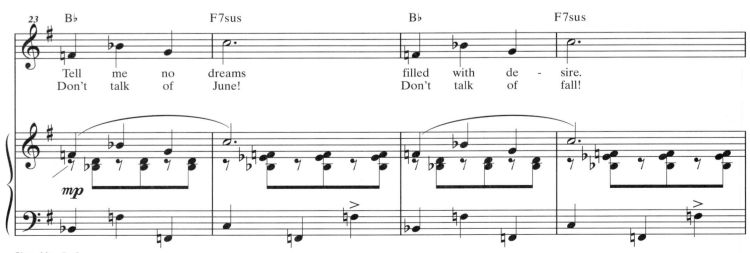

Show Me - 5 - 2
32766

WITHOUT YOU
(from "My Fair Lady")

Words by
ALAN JAY LERNER

Music by
FREDERICK LOEWE

Allegro con anima

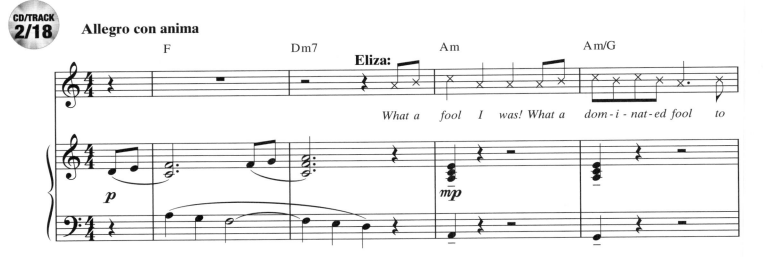

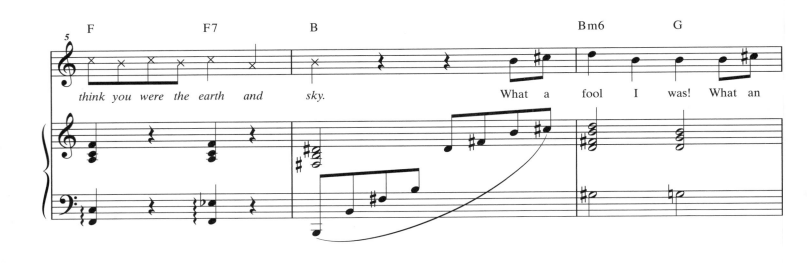

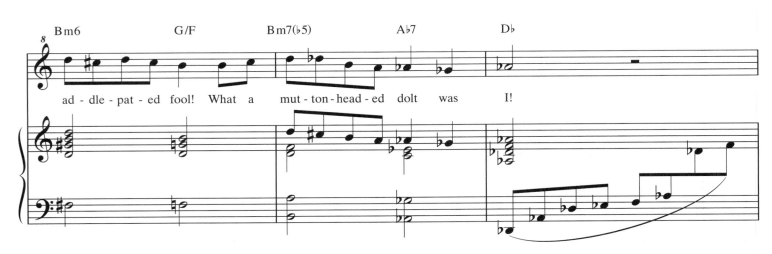

Without You - 6 - 1
32766

Tempo I

not feel a-lone with-out you. I can

stand on my own with-out you._____ So go back in your shell, I can

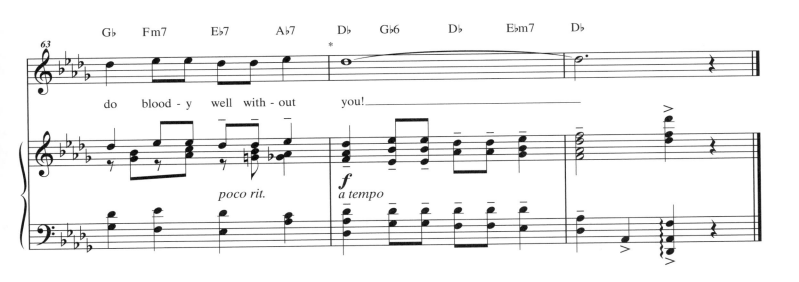

do blood-y well with-out you!_____

poco rit.   *a tempo*

*In the show version, Henry Higgins interrupts the song at this point and ends the piece with a brief sixteen-bar section.
We've eliminated Higgins' part, and included a short two-bar ending to complete ths song.

SOMEONE TO WATCH OVER ME

(from "Oh, Kay!")

Music and Lyrics by
GEORGE GERSHWIN and IRA GERSHWIN

Someone to Watch Over Me - 4 - 1
32766

THE HUMAN HEART

(from "Once on This Island")

Lyrics by
LYNN AHRENS

Music by
STEPHEN FLAHERTY

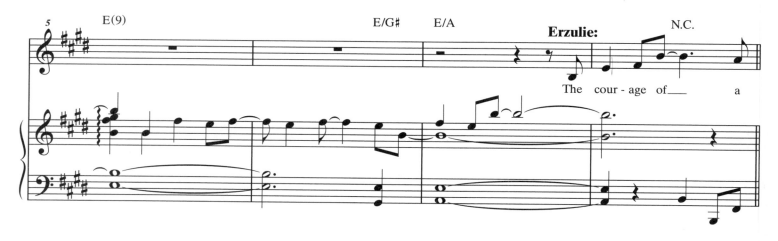

The Human Heart - 6 - 1
32766

WAITING FOR LIFE

(from "Once on This Island")

Lyrics by
LYNN AHRENS

Music by
STEPHEN FLAHERTY

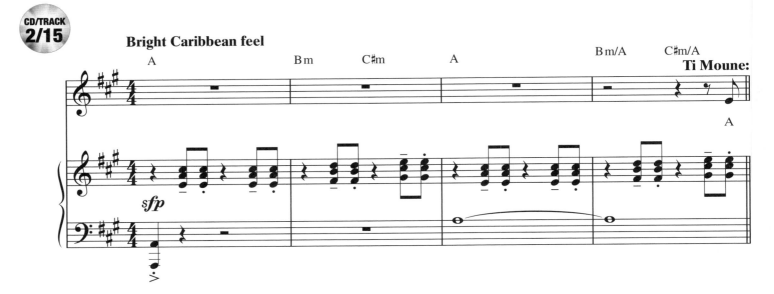

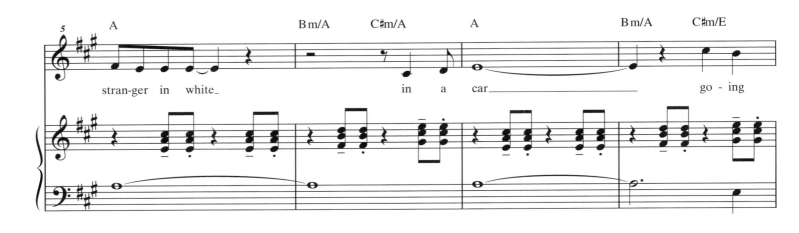

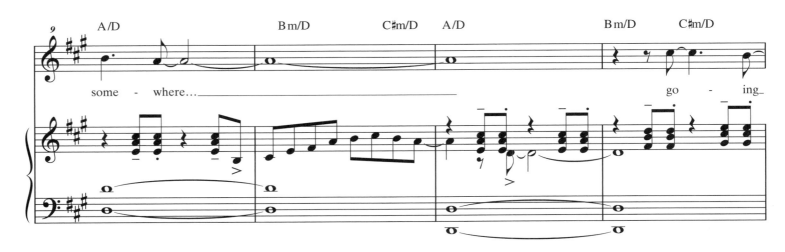

get me! _____ Oh, gods! Oh, __ gods, __ let me

fly! _____ Send me to plac - es where no ___ one be - fore __ me has

been. _____ You spared my __ life, _____ show me
(Oo - la, oo - la, oo - la!)

why _____ you get me to rise __ like a fish __ to the bait, __ then

WHAT IS A MAN?
(from "Pal Joey")

Words by
LORENZ HART

Music by
RICHARD RODGERS

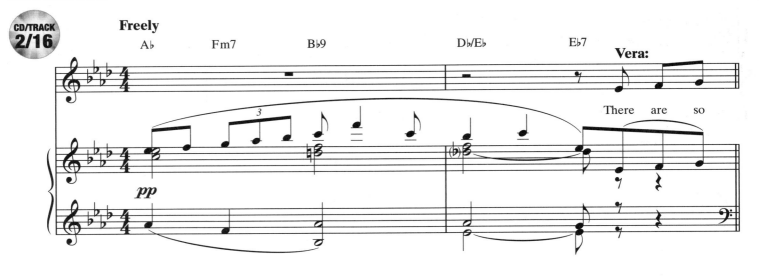

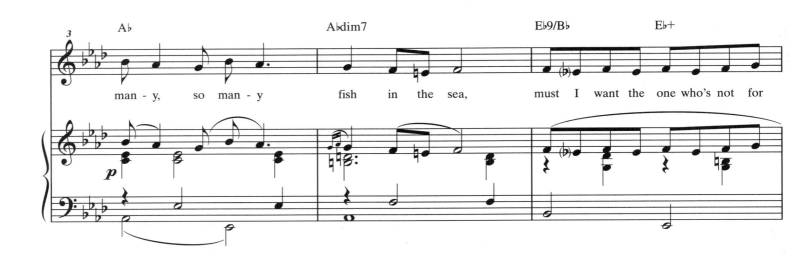

What Is a Man? - 6 - 1
32766

much too used to love to be with-out it.   What   is   a

man?   Is   he   an   an-i-mal?   Is   he   a   wolf,

is   he   a   mouse?   Is   he   the   cheap   or   the   dear   kind?____

____   Is   he   cham-pagne   or   the   beer   kind?_____

164

What Is a Man? - 6 - 3
32766

BEWITCHED, BOTHERED AND BEWILDERED

(from "Pal Joey")

Words by
LORENZ HART

Music by
RICHARD RODGERS

Moderately slow, with expression (♩ = 60)

Refrain:

FORTY DAYS

(from "Passion")

Music and Lyrics by
STEPHEN SONDHEIM

I'm fill-ing up the room, our lit-tle room, with ev-'ry flow-er in bloom. I'll have the

fi - re lit, the ta-ble set, I'll wear the blue chem - ise._____ And once we're in our

room, our se-cret room, where I'll be a - ble to care for you,

kiss you, em - brace you, be there for you.

(Train whistle)

ff

SUMMERTIME
(from "Porgy and Bess" ®)

Words and Music by
GEORGE GERSHWIN,
DuBOSE and DOROTHY HEYWARD
and IRA GERSHWIN

Allegretto semplice

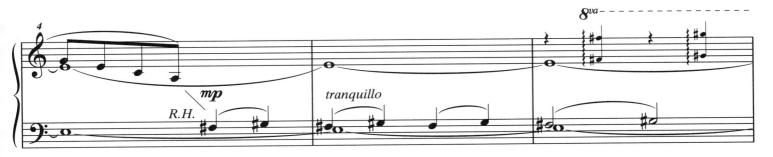

Moderately, with expression (♩ = 40)

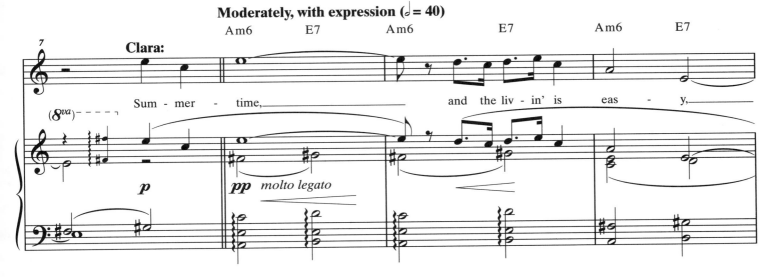

Sum - mer - time, _____ and the liv - in' is eas - y, _____

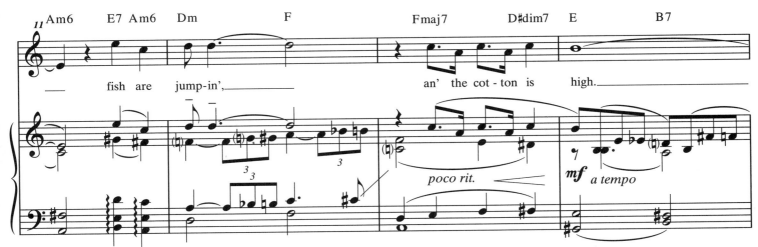

fish are jump - in', _____ an' the cot - ton is high. _____

Summertime - 3 - 1
32766

LEAVIN' FOR THE PROMISE' LAN'

(from "Porgy and Bess" ®)

Words and Music by
GEORGE GERSHWIN,
DuBOSE and DOROTHY HEYWARD
and IRA GERSHWIN

Andantino quasi marcia funebre (♩ = 69)

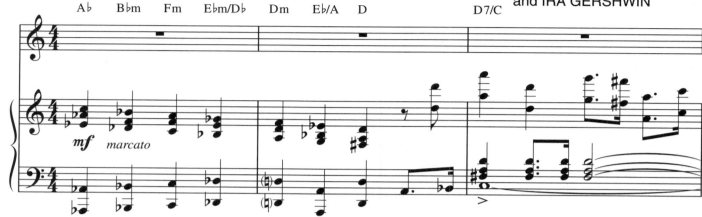

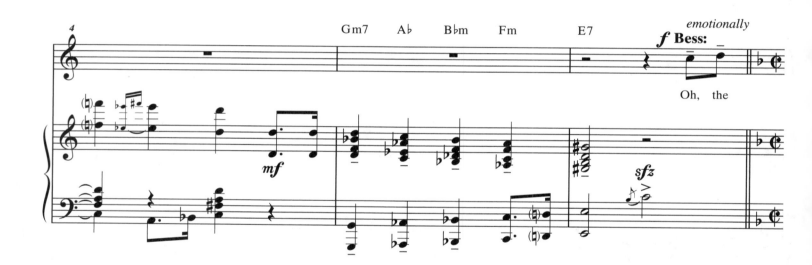

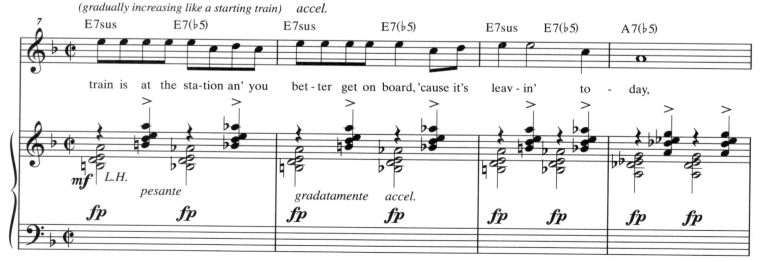

COME TO MY GARDEN
(from "The Secret Garden")

Lyrics by
MARSHA NORMAN

Music by
LUCY SIMON

*Lily:

Come to my gar - den nes - tled in the hill.

There I'll keep you safe be - side me.

Come to my gar - den, rest there in my arms.

* This solo by Lily is excerpted from the complete song version in the show.

Come to My Garden - 2 - 1
32766

HOW COULD I EVER KNOW?

(from "The Secret Garden")

Lyrics by
MARSHA NORMAN

Music by
LUCY SIMON

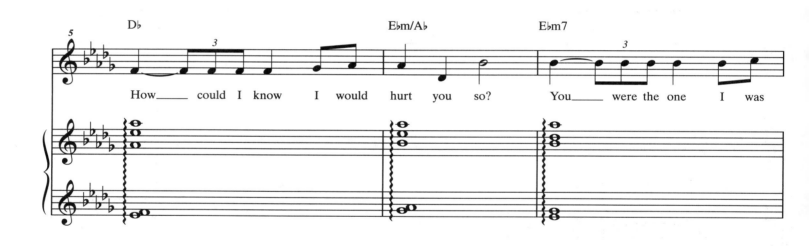

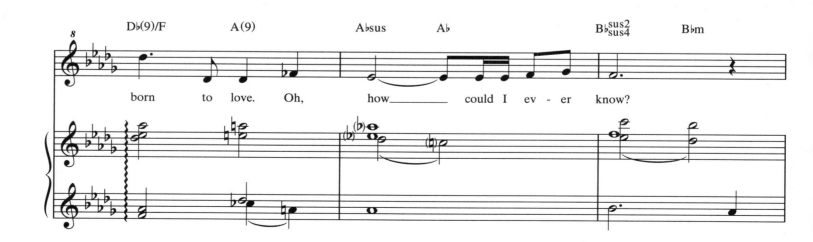

How Could I Ever Know? - 4 - 1
32766

Andante con moto

Più mosso

Più passionato

THE MAN I LOVE
(from "Strike Up the Band")

Music and Lyrics by
GEORGE GERSHWIN and IRA GERSHWIN

HANGIN' AROUND WITH YOU

(from "Strike Up the Band")

Music and Lyrics by
GEORGE GERSHWIN and IRA GERSHWIN

GREEN FINCH AND LINNET BIRD

(from "Sweeney Todd")

Music and Lyrics by
STEPHEN SONDHEIM

Notes

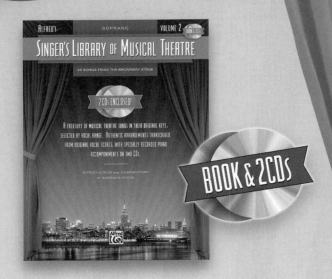